Turn your dreams into reality

The $2 Million Journey

My Modest Success in the Financial Products Industry

A Path Anyone Can Follow

Randhir Bhalla

Dedication

This book is dedicated to all those with an unwavering commitment to building wealth through the most reliable paths.

I am profoundly grateful to my mentors, who, at the onset of my journey, provided invaluable guidance and illuminated a path toward achieving wealth and success with honesty, integrity, and minimal risk.

Table of Contents

Preface

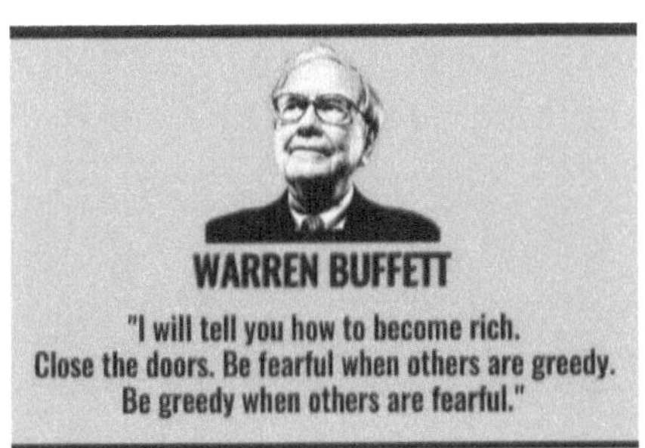

There could not have been a more fitting time to write this book, starting with the iconic quote by Warren Buffett. The global financial markets are currently experiencing unprecedented chaos. The Sensex has plummeted over 16% from its peak, while mid-cap and small-cap indexes have fallen by 21% and 25%, respectively. Additionally, more than 90% of Sensex stocks are trading below their 200-day moving average (DMA), signalling a prolonged downward trend.

In such uncertain times, offering guidance on wealth accumulation becomes a daunting task. It is precisely in moments like these that Warren Buffett's wisdom serves as a beacon of hope. His famous quote, as depicted in this book, resonates deeply with my personal investment journey.

Having navigated numerous financial downturns myself, I have learned that hidden within every crisis lies an opportunity – an opportunity that most fail to recognize amidst fear and doubt. This book aims to share those lessons and provide practical tips on how to accumulate wealth even during turbulent times.

Read this book with conviction, apply its insights, and you will be better equipped to create a prosperous future.

May God bless you on your journey.

About the Author

Randhir Bhalla & Associates is a distinguished firm composed of seasoned professionals, including Senior Engineers, Chartered Accountants, and Cost and Management Accountants. Leading this accomplished team is Randhir Bhalla, an esteemed author and authority in his field.

Due to his profound expertise and impactful contributions, Randhir has been invited to speak at prestigious events organized by respected institutions, including FICCI (Federation of Indian Chambers of Commerce & Industry), ASSOCHAM (Associated Chambers of Commerce and Industry of India) in New Delhi, and FKCCI (Federation of Karnataka Chambers of Commerce & Industry) in Bengaluru.

Widely regarded as an expert in Financial Business Continuity Planning across India, Randhir has developed customized Financial Business Continuity Plans that are invaluable assets to business enterprises, their promoters, collaborators, investors, and key personnel. His core philosophy, that Protection (P) always surpasses Returns (R), underscores the importance of robust risk management. With his unique approach, Randhir skilfully designs comprehensive Risk Protection plans for HNIs, helping them mitigate risks effectively and enjoy peace of mind.

The Author's Previous Books

He has written 4 notable books that offer invaluable insights into the world of insurance sales and wealth-building strategies:

1. **"6 Secrets of Selling 100 Cr (1 Billion) Insurance to HNIs with Ease"** – In this book, Randhir shares proven strategies for effectively selling high-value insurance policies to High Net Worth Individuals (HNIs). He provides readers with the insights needed to navigate this exclusive market confidently and achieve substantial success.

2. **"Sell Big Insurance to Unknown Ferrari Owners"** – Focused on the niche of insuring luxury vehicle owners, this book explores unique techniques for reaching and serving clients with high-end assets, such as Ferraris. Randhir provides a fresh perspective on capturing this specialized segment and maximizing growth potential.

3. **"How to Make a Million Dollars in the Insurance Business No Matter How Bad the Economy Is"** – Drawing from his extensive experience, Randhir shares practical wisdom on attaining financial success even in challenging economic times. He outlines actionable strategies that enable readers to generate significant wealth through resilience and skilful business practices.

4. **"Unlocking Big Ticket Insurance and Mutual Fund Sales"** - In this book, Randhir Bhalla provides actionable strategies for insurance agents to adapt to industry changes, including the introduction of Jeevan Sugam and rising competition from online platforms. Emphasizing innovation and

diversification into mutual funds, debt, and equity products, the book equips professionals to meet the evolving needs of sophisticated clients and achieve lasting success in the financial sector.

📞 **Contact Us:**
✉ **Email:** randhirbhalla1950@gmail.com
📱 **Mobile:** +91 9376117563 / +91 8141117563

About the Book

This is truly amazing! Indians are living longer than ever.

Year vs. Average Life Span in India

- **1900** → 25.4 years
- **1947** → 31 years
- **1951** → 37.1 years
- **2000** → 62.2 years
- **2021** → 67.3 years
- **2024** → 72.24 years

This is a crucial wake-up call for anyone who hasn't started planning for retirement.
The key to a secure and enjoyable retirement is to start saving consistently and making smart investments today.

Wealth-building is not as complex or out of reach as it may seem—anyone, regardless of background or experience, can attain it. The core principles are simple and widely understood. Save consistently, invest thoughtfully, avoid unnecessary debt, and maintain a long-term perspective. The real challenge lies not in these concepts themselves, but in the desire to achieve wealth RAPIDLY.

This book is not written to celebrate the author's personal success; rather, it is a practical guide inspired by the author's experience. He recognizes that countless others have achieved remarkable financial milestones, some even greater, within similar timeframes. The primary purpose here is to educate—to illustrate that by consistently following foundational investment principles, anyone can achieve financial results that many only dreams of.

Through this journey, the author aspires to empower readers to apply these strategies, proving that sound investment practices are within reach for anyone eager to learn and act. With commitment and knowledge, readers can transform financial aspirations into tangible success.

Chapter - 1
A Real-Life Story: Mr. Shah vs. Mr. Patel

A few years ago, I heard a story from Mr. Nilesh Shah, Managing Director at Kotak Mahindra Asset Management, which manages assets worth over ₹44,000 crore. This story left a lasting impression on me as it highlighted the importance of taking calculated risks in investments and choosing the right asset allocation to build wealth without unnecessary fear and anxiety.

The Story

Twenty years ago, Mr. Nilesh Shah knew two individuals with vastly different financial mindsets and approaches to investment.

Mr. Shah was a wealthy man who enjoyed a luxurious lifestyle, including a chauffeur-driven Mercedes. In contrast, Mr. Patel was a middle-class man with a modest income, commuting on a Bajaj scooter.

Being highly conservative, Mr. Shah avoided any form of financial risk and invested all his savings in debt-related funds, which offered a meagre pre-tax return of 7-8%. On the other hand, Mr. Patel was more financially savvy. He sought the advice of a seasoned financial advisor and adopted a balanced investment strategy—allocating his funds between equity and debt instruments.

For years, both men continued on their respective investment paths without wavering from their chosen strategies.

The Turning Point

After two decades, Mr. Nilesh Shah happened to meet both of them at a wedding. What he saw shocked him—their financial positions had completely reversed.

Mr. Patel, the once middle-class man, arrived in a brand-new chauffeur-driven Mercedes, while Mr. Shah, the former wealthy man, now drove an old Maruti model.

The Diagnosis

The reason behind this dramatic reversal was simple:

- Mr. Shah's conservative investment approach kept him in low-yield debt funds, earning post-tax returns of merely 4-5%. These returns failed to outpace inflation, which gradually eroded his wealth and forced him to downgrade his lifestyle.
- Mr. Patel, on the other hand, made intelligent investment choices. By consistently investing in equity while maintaining a small portion in debt, he achieved an average return of 15%, significantly outpacing inflation.
- The power of **compounding** worked in Mr. Patel's favour, steadily growing his wealth over time and transforming his financial status.

The Lesson

This story profoundly influenced my perspective on wealth creation. It reinforced my belief in the importance of strategic risk-taking and asset allocation to secure financial prosperity.

To dive deeper into these principles and understand how you can apply them to your own financial journey, continue reading this book.

Chapter - 2
From My Own Journey,
I Offer These Insights:

a) Building Wealth Isn't Inherently Difficult; the Challenge Lies in Doing It Quickly

Building wealth is not a complex or unattainable goal—it's something that anyone, regardless of background or experience, can achieve. In fact, the basic principles of wealth-building are straightforward and well-known: save regularly, invest wisely, avoid debt, and plan for the long term. However, what makes the process seem difficult is not the concept itself, but the challenge of achieving wealth quickly.

Over the years, I've learned that the real difficulty in building wealth quickly lies in overcoming common obstacles and implementing strategies that accelerate the process. From my own journey, here's how I've come to understand why speed is challenging and how it can be achieved:

1. The Need for Discipline and Consistency Over Time

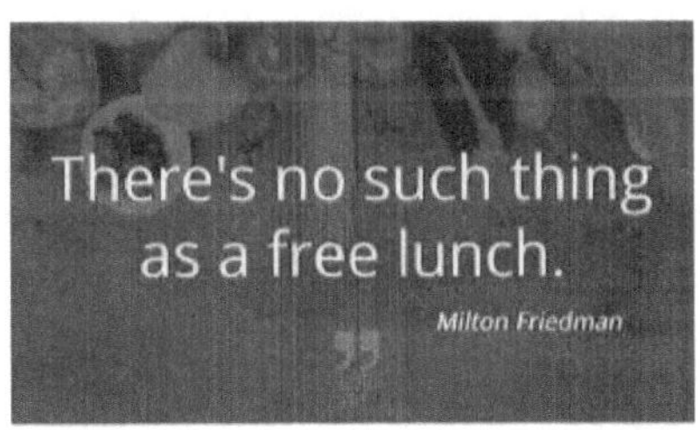

"There's no such thing as a free lunch." You need to earn it by staying disciplined.

While the principles of wealth-building are simple, sticking to them over time with discipline and consistency is where most people struggle. The challenge of building wealth quickly isn't about understanding the process, but rather having the self-control to avoid distractions and emotional decisions. Too often, people want instant gratification or are lured by the idea of "get rich quick" schemes, which leads to mistakes and missed opportunities.

I've learned that success isn't about making impulsive, high-risk moves but rather about making steady, well-thought-out decisions over time. The key lies in developing habits that become second nature—like consistently contributing to your savings or investment accounts, even when the market is uncertain. This disciplined approach is what drives long-term wealth-building. The real challenge is staying committed, especially when the results aren't immediately visible.

2. Harnessing the Power of Compounding

Albert Einstein is often credited with saying, *"Compound interest is the eighth wonder of the world. He who understands it, earns it. He who doesn't, pays it".*

The real power behind wealth-building is compounding—the ability for your investments to earn returns not just on the principal amount you invested, but also on the accumulated returns. Compounding is a game-changer, and it's one of the reasons why starting early is so important. But the key to accelerating wealth-building lies in consistently reinvesting profits back into your investments, rather than pulling them out prematurely.

In the early years of my journey, I focused on making smart, disciplined investments and then allowed the power of compounding to take effect. It wasn't about making a huge amount of money overnight, but instead allowing time to do the work for me. The challenge in building wealth quickly is not the act of investing itself but staying patient and disciplined enough to let compounding deliver its benefits.

3. Identifying and Seizing Opportunities

Building wealth quickly requires you to identify and capitalize on opportunities that align with your long-term goals. While traditional wealth-building strategies such as saving regularly and investing in equities are essential, being able to spot opportunities that will give you an accelerated return is equally important. These opportunities may come in the form of high-growth sectors, new technologies, or niche investments that others overlook.

I've seen firsthand how important it is to constantly scan the market and seek out these opportunities. For example, early investments in emerging sectors, such as technology or renewable energy, can provide returns far above the market average. However, this requires not just a good understanding of the market but also a willingness to take calculated risks. The challenge in building wealth quickly is having the foresight and courage to act on these opportunities before they become mainstream.

4. Leveraging Debt to Build Wealth

Another key factor in building wealth quickly is knowing how to leverage debt effectively.

While debt can be a double-edged sword, using it wisely can accelerate your wealth-building journey. For example, using a mortgage to purchase property or taking out low-interest loans to invest in income-generating assets can help you grow your wealth faster than relying solely on your savings.

However, the challenge is knowing when and how to use debt strategically without overextending yourself. It's about understanding the balance between using debt to fuel growth while maintaining enough financial flexibility to weather downturns. I've learned that leveraging debt in the right way allows you to accelerate wealth accumulation—but doing so wisely and cautiously is crucial.

5. Building Multiple Income Streams

One of the most important lessons I learned in my journey was that relying on a single source of income makes the process of building wealth much slower. To build wealth quickly, you need to create multiple streams of income—whether through investments, side businesses, or other opportunities.

This diversification ensures that your wealth-building efforts aren't tied to just one source of income, and it accelerates the process by increasing the total amount of capital that's working for you.

I focused on diversifying my income early on, creating not just active income from my work but also passive income from investments in stocks, real estate, and other ventures. The challenge in accelerating wealth-building is figuring out how to juggle multiple income streams while ensuring that they are well-managed and aligned with your overall goals.

6. The Role of Risk-Taking

Mark Zuckerberg, the co-founder of Facebook, said, "The biggest risk is not taking any risk".

Building wealth quickly often involves taking calculated risks. Unlike traditional wealth-building, which focuses on gradual accumulation and long-term stability, fast wealth-building strategies often involve a willingness to take higher risks. These risks can include investing in new or speculative ventures, taking on more leverage, or exploring high-reward opportunities.

However, this doesn't mean reckless gambling. Instead, the challenge lies in learning how to take smart, well-researched risks.

Over the years, I've taken calculated risks by investing in emerging markets or innovative products before they became mainstream. The challenge in wealth-building is knowing when to take the leap and when to wait, but always ensuring that you are making decisions based on data and research, not emotion.

7. Avoiding the Pitfalls of Short-Term Thinking

One of the most difficult aspects of building wealth quickly is the temptation to focus on short-term gains. The financial world is full of trends that promise immediate results, but these are often fleeting and can lead to poor decision-making. In my journey, I learned that true wealth is not built through impulsive or speculative moves, but through a combination of strategic patience and timely action.

The challenge is staying focused on long-term financial goals, even when there are enticing short-term opportunities. Building wealth quickly requires being able to assess opportunities from a long-term perspective while still acting quickly enough to seize them.

8. Emotional Control and Avoiding Impulse Decisions

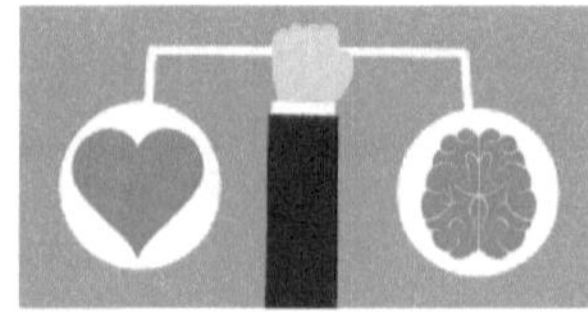

One of the most significant hurdles in building wealth quickly is emotional control. The financial markets are filled with uncertainty, volatility, and temptation. Fear and greed are two emotions that can derail an otherwise sound wealth-building strategy. Early in my journey, I learned the importance of making decisions based on logic and analysis, rather than giving in to fear during market dips or chasing profits during bull markets.

The challenge lies in developing the mental discipline to stay focused and not react impulsively to market fluctuations. Keeping a cool head, sticking to your strategy, and making decisions based on data, not emotions, is key to accelerating wealth-building.

Conclusion: Building Wealth Quickly is a Matter of Strategy and Discipline

Building wealth itself is not inherently difficult—what makes it challenging is accelerating the process. It requires a blend of knowledge, discipline, strategic risk-taking, and emotional control.

The key to success lies in leveraging the time you have, making informed decisions, and staying disciplined in your approach. While the journey may be challenging, the rewards of financial independence and wealth-building are well worth the effort, and with the right approach, you can achieve financial success much faster than you might think.

Chapter - 3
From My Own Journey, I Offer These Insights:

b) The process of wealth creation is 99% about mindset and temperament, and only 1% intelligence.

The process of wealth creation is overwhelmingly influenced by one's mindset and temperament, contributing to about 99% of the journey, while intelligence plays a smaller role, accounting for just 1%. This perspective underscores the importance of psychological and emotional factors over pure cognitive abilities in achieving financial success.

A resilient and positive mindset is essential for overcoming the inevitable challenges and setbacks in wealth building. It cultivates perseverance, allowing individuals to stay focused on long-term financial goals despite short-term fluctuations and uncertainties. This mindset is built on disciplined saving and investing, a commitment to continuous learning, and the flexibility to adapt to changing market conditions.

Temperament also plays a critical role, especially in how one reacts to stress and financial risk. A balanced

temperament helps maintain focus and objectivity, preventing emotional decision-making that can lead to poor financial choices. This ability to remain composed and pragmatic in all situations, much like a YOGI who embodies Stitha Pragnya (a state of profound and balanced judgement), is crucial for making strategic decisions that align with one's financial goals.

In contrast, intelligence, while useful, is only a small part of the equation. It can aid in understanding complex financial instruments and markets, but without the right mindset and temperament, even the most intelligent individuals can struggle to achieve and sustain wealth. This highlights that success in wealth creation is less about technical knowledge and more about psychological resilience and emotional intelligence.

Chapter - 4
From My Own Journey,
I Offer These Insights:

c) Adopt a mindset akin to a YOGI—remain balanced through life's ups and downs and stay committed to your long-term vision.

Adopting a mindset similar to that of a YOGI— characterized by balance and steadiness through life's ups and downs—is crucial for long-term success in wealth creation. This philosophy emphasizes maintaining a calm and centred disposition, regardless of external circumstances, which is vital in navigating the volatile realms of investing and wealth management.

A YOGI-like mindset involves cultivating deep self-awareness and discipline, which allows individuals to detach from short-term market fluctuations and emotional impulses that can lead to rash decisions. By remaining emotionally balanced, one can more effectively adhere to a strategic financial plan without being swayed by the fear or greed that often disrupts the investment decisions of less disciplined investors.

Staying committed to a long-term vision is another key aspect of this mindset. It requires a clear understanding of one's financial goals and the patience to see through long-term investments, even when they perform poorly in the short term. This long-view approach ensures that decisions are made with a focus on eventual outcomes, rather than immediate gains, which often leads to more sustainable wealth accumulation.

Furthermore, this YOGI mindset encourages a holistic approach to life and finances. It fosters a lifestyle that is not only focused on financial accumulation but also on personal growth, health, and well-being. This balanced lifestyle helps mitigate stress and maintain the mental clarity needed to make informed financial decisions, thus supporting a sustainable path to achieving and maintaining wealth.

Chapter - 5
From My Own Journey, I Offer These Insights:

d) Simplicity in Your Approach Can Lead to More Effective Wealth Creation

Sometimes, the best investment action is no action at all.

When it comes to building wealth, there's often a misconception that complexity is the key to success. Many people believe that intricate strategies, high-risk investments, and constant market analysis are necessary to achieve financial freedom. However, based on my own experience, I've found that simplicity is not only effective—it's often the most powerful approach for long-term wealth creation. Here's why a simple, focused strategy can be your most reliable path to financial success.

1. The Power of Focused Goals

The first step toward effective wealth creation is having clear and focused financial goals. The simplicity of setting concrete, measurable goals allow you to streamline your efforts and avoid distractions. Instead of trying to chase every opportunity or investment that crosses your path, simplicity encourages you to focus on the essentials—what really matters in the long run.

For instance, when I started out, I made it my goal to achieve financial independence within a set number of years. I didn't complicate my plan by jumping into too many different markets or trying to pursue every new trend. I knew my goal, and I kept my strategy simple: save consistently, invest wisely, and reinvest profits. By keeping my focus on this straightforward plan, I could maintain a steady course and avoid the noise of short-term fluctuations.

2. Simplifying Your Investment Strategy

One of the biggest advantages of simplicity in wealth creation is the clarity it provides in your investment strategy. You don't need a complicated portfolio filled with a mix of exotic assets, high-risk investments, and countless derivatives to build wealth. In fact, a simple, diversified portfolio of well-researched, stable assets can provide you with more than enough growth potential over time.

I personally focused on a few solid asset classes—equities, bonds, and real estate—because they aligned with my long-term goals and offered consistent returns with relatively low complexity. Over time, I added other low-maintenance investments such as dividend-paying stocks and index funds. By avoiding overly complex investments or constantly trying to time the market, I ensured that my portfolio remained manageable and focused on growth without the stress of excessive trading or speculation.

3. Reducing Risk with a Simple, Diversified Approach

Simplicity does not mean ignoring risk—it means understanding and mitigating it in a way that's easy to manage. A simple approach to wealth creation often involves diversification, but without over-complicating the portfolio. For example, I focused on ensuring that my investments were spread across different sectors and asset classes, but I didn't go overboard by investing in too many niche markets or speculative ventures.

By diversifying my investments into core assets like real estate, broad-market mutual funds, and stocks, I minimized risk without overextending myself. I didn't feel the need to track hundreds of small, speculative investments. Instead, I kept my strategy simple, spreading my investments across different, stable opportunities that were aligned with my risk tolerance and financial goals.

The beauty of this simple diversification strategy is that it allows you to take advantage of market growth while reducing exposure to any single, high-risk asset. In the long run, this can protect your wealth and lead to more sustainable growth.

4. Saving and Investing Regularly Over Time

Another key to simplicity is consistency. Building wealth doesn't require complex strategies—it requires the discipline to save and invest regularly.

The simple act of putting money aside each month, even in small amounts, allows you to gradually build wealth over time. In fact, consistent contributions over time often produce better results than trying to time the market or make big, infrequent investments.

In my journey, I made a habit of setting aside a fixed percentage of my income each month for investments. I didn't worry about trying to time the market or whether the market was up or down. I focused on the process—staying consistent and ensuring that I was always investing towards my long-term goals. Over time, this regular habit became the cornerstone of my wealth creation strategy. By keeping it simple and disciplined, I was able to steadily build a growing portfolio.

5. Letting Time Work for You Through Compounding

The concept of compounding is one of the most straightforward yet powerful tools in wealth creation. When you keep things simple and invest regularly, your returns compound over time, meaning you earn returns on both your initial investment and the returns it generates. The longer your money stays invested, the more significant the effect of compounding becomes.

In my case, I made sure that any returns or dividends I received were reinvested back into my portfolio. This simple act of reinvesting profits allowed the magic of compounding to accelerate my wealth. Instead of complicating matters by pulling money out or making complex adjustments to my portfolio, I trusted the power of compounding and allowed my investments to grow naturally over time.

6. Avoiding the Distraction of Speculation

A common pitfall for many investors is getting caught up in speculative opportunities that seem to promise quick profits. While complex strategies, high-risk investments, or chasing speculative bubbles may seem exciting, they often come with high levels of risk that undermine long-term wealth creation. Keeping things simple means avoiding these distractions and staying focused on stable, reliable investments that align with your goals.

I've seen firsthand how easy it is to get pulled into "hot" opportunities—whether that's chasing a promising stock, investing in a trend, or buying into high-risk speculation. However, I always kept my eye on the bigger picture, resisting the temptation to chase quick wins and instead sticking to solid investments that I understood well. This simplicity in focus allowed me to avoid making impulsive decisions and instead build wealth in a way that was both consistent and sustainable.

7. Reducing Stress and Gaining Clarity

Simplicity also plays a vital role in reducing the stress and complexity that can often accompany wealth creation. The financial markets are full of uncertainty, and trying to manage a portfolio of complex, high-risk assets can lead to sleepless nights and emotional decisions. By keeping things simple, you can gain clarity and peace of mind, knowing that your financial strategy is easy to manage and aligned with your long-term goals.

When you adopt a simple approach, you reduce the need for constant monitoring of investments or worrying about every market fluctuation. With a clear, straightforward strategy in place, you're better able to stay calm and focused, even when the markets are volatile. This reduces the emotional stress of managing wealth and gives you the mental clarity needed to make sound financial decisions.

8. Long-Term Sustainability and Growth

The key to creating lasting wealth is sustainability. Simplicity in your approach fosters long-term sustainability, as it allows you to maintain a steady course without getting sidetracked by short-term trends or complicated financial instruments. Wealth creation is not a sprint; it's a marathon. The more straightforward and consistent your approach, the more likely it is that you will build wealth over time and avoid the pitfalls that derail many investors.

By focusing on simple strategies that can be consistently applied over many years, you are more likely to create wealth that lasts. This allows you to not only achieve financial success, but to maintain it and pass it on to future generations, which is ultimately the goal of true wealth creation.

Conclusion: Simple Strategies Lead to Powerful Results

Building wealth doesn't have to be complicated. In fact, simplicity often leads to more effective and sustainable wealth creation. By focusing on clear goals, consistent investing, diversification, and the power of compounding, you can achieve financial success without getting bogged down by unnecessary complexity. By following a simple, disciplined approach to wealth creation, you can accelerate your financial journey and build lasting prosperity.

Chapter - 6
The Best Time Is Yet to Come: India's Bright Future in the Stock Market

When asked about the best time to invest in the stock market in India, Mr. Radhakrishnan Damani, a veteran stock market dealer and the promoter of D-Mart, whose personal net worth is over ₹70,000 crore ($8300 Million), gave a simple yet powerful response:

"The next 20 years."

This statement isn't just the opinion of one individual; it reflects the broader sentiment shared by numerous experts who believe that India is uniquely positioned for massive growth over the next two decades. Let's explore why this period is considered one of the most exciting times to invest in India's financial markets and why setbacks, although inevitable, will not derail the country's long-term upward trajectory.

1. India's Rapid Economic Growth

India is already one of the fastest-growing economies in the world, and its economic expansion is expected to continue for many years. The country's GDP growth has remained robust, even in the face of global challenges. India's demographic advantage, with a young and growing workforce, has created a fertile ground for innovation, entrepreneurship, and job creation. Furthermore, the government's focus on infrastructure development, digital transformation, and the ease of doing business has contributed significantly to the country's economic progress.

Over the next two decades, India is poised to become the world's third-largest economy, overtaking major players like Japan and Germany. This growth will inevitably drive demand across various sectors, including technology, healthcare, consumer goods, real estate, and financial services. The growth of India's middle class, along with rising disposable incomes, will further fuel demand for a wide range of products and services, leading to the expansion of Indian businesses and creating wealth for investors.

2. Setbacks and Resilience: Lessons from the Past

Mr. Damani's remark about setbacks highlights a crucial point: setbacks are a natural part of any market or economy. What's more important is how the country and its market participants respond to these challenges. India's history is replete with challenges that seemed insurmountable at the time, yet the country has always bounced back stronger, with its economy and stock market consistently recovering and reaching new heights.

3. The 1990s Economic Crisis and Reforms

In the early 1990s, India faced a severe balance of payments crisis, resulting in the country's government taking bold measures to liberalize the economy. The introduction of economic reforms in 1991, including reducing trade barriers, promoting foreign investments, and privatizing state-owned companies, paved the way for India's economic ascent. The stock market, which had been largely inaccessible to the average Indian investor, grew exponentially in the following decades.

4. The Dot-Com Bubble and Global Financial Crisis

The 2000s were marked by the bursting of the dot-com bubble, followed by the global financial crisis (GFC) of 2008. India, like the rest of the world, felt the impact of these events. However, despite the short-term turbulence in the stock market, India's long-term economic fundamentals remained intact. The country's stock market rebounded strongly in the years following the crisis, with the Sensex and Nifty indices climbing to new highs. Companies that had adapted to global changes and focused on innovation thrived during this period, rewarding investors who remained patient and focused on the long-term horizon.

5. The COVID-19 Pandemic

The COVID-19 pandemic was another major setback that affected the global economy, leading to a sharp downturn in stock markets worldwide. India's stock market was not immune to this shock, but the recovery post-pandemic has been nothing short of remarkable. The government's stimulus packages,

along with the rapid vaccination campaign, helped revive consumer confidence and industrial production. Many sectors, including technology, e-commerce, pharmaceuticals, and renewable energy, have seen tremendous growth since the pandemic, proving the resilience of the Indian market.

Chapter - 7
India's Bright Future: Key Drivers of Growth

India's long-term growth story is not just about recovering from past setbacks but about the enduring factors that will continue to drive its economic and market growth:

1. Demographic Dividend

India's population of over 1.4 billion people includes a large percentage of young individuals who are entering the workforce. This demographic dividend provides a powerful engine for growth, as a youthful population leads to higher productivity, greater innovation, and increased consumption. As more young people achieve higher levels of education and gain skills in emerging industries, India will continue to fuel its economic expansion.

2. Digital Transformation

India's digital transformation is already underway, with the country emerging as one of the world's largest digital economies. The government's push for a digital India, along with the rise of fintech, e-commerce, and mobile technology, is creating new opportunities for businesses and investors alike. The digital economy's growth, combined with the rapid adoption of technology in various sectors, including

education, healthcare, and manufacturing, will
continue to drive the economy forward.

3. Infrastructure Development

The Indian government has made significant strides
in improving infrastructure, ranging from
transportation networks to energy production. The
focus on improving roads, railways, ports, and
airports will enable better connectivity, reduce costs,
and increase productivity across the economy.
Moreover, the development of smart cities and
urbanization will create new investment opportunities
for real estate developers and infrastructure
companies.

4. Globalization and Trade Agreements

India's integration into the global economy is
expected to deepen over the next two decades. As the
world moves toward more diversified supply chains
and regional trade agreements, India's role as a
manufacturing hub and trade partner will continue to
grow. The government's efforts to negotiate trade
agreements with various countries and regions will
open new markets for Indian companies and
investors.

5. Environmental Sustainability

Sustainability is becoming a major theme in India's development. The country has committed to ambitious goals for renewable energy production, including becoming a leader in solar power. As India moves toward a green economy, there will be opportunities for investment in clean energy, electric vehicles, and other environmentally friendly technologies. These sectors will see rapid growth, driven by both government policy and market demand.

Chapter - 8
The Road Ahead: Opportunities and Risks

While the next 20 years hold immense promise, it is important for investors to understand that setbacks are inevitable. As history has shown, market volatility and economic challenges will arise, but the long-term growth trajectory of India remains strong. The key is to approach investing with a long-term mindset, recognizing that short-term dips are merely temporary obstacles on the path to wealth creation.

By investing with a disciplined, patient approach, understanding market cycles, and focusing on sectors with strong growth potential, investors can position themselves to take advantage of India's bright future. The best time to invest in India's stock market may very well be right now, as the country embarks on a journey of growth that will continue for decades to come.

Conclusion: A Bright Future for India's Economy and Stock Market

India is at a critical juncture, with unprecedented opportunities on the horizon. The next 20 years promise to be a period of rapid economic growth, fuelled by demographic changes, technological advancements, and infrastructure development. While setbacks will come, India's history of resilience and its current trajectory suggest that the future is brighter than ever for investors willing to stay the course.

Mr. Radhakrishnan Damani's belief that the next two decades will be the best time to invest in India is shared by many experts in the industry. The Indian stock market, which has already weathered numerous challenges and emerged stronger each time, is poised for even greater growth in the coming years. For those looking to create long-term wealth, the time to invest in India is now—and the best is yet to come.

Chapter - 9
From Rs. 10 Lacs to Rs. 100 Cr in 30 Years: The Power of Compounding and Smart Investing

It might sound almost too good to be true turning an initial investment of Rs. 10 lakhs into Rs. 100 crores in just 30 years. However, this scenario isn't based on some get-rich-quick scheme; it's a result of strategic investing, compounding returns, and the power of choosing high-growth opportunities over time. While this journey from Rs. 10 lakhs to Rs. 100 crores might seem "weird" at first glance, let's break it down and show how this financial magic is entirely possible with the right approach.

The Magic of Doubling Every 3 Years

Imagine you invested Rs. 10 lakhs in a company whose profits double every 3 years. If this rate of growth can be sustained for a long period, your investment can experience extraordinary returns. When your investments grow at a rate of 22% per year, they double in value approximately every three years.

Let's see how this works in practice:

- After 3 years, your Rs. 10 lakh investment grows to Rs. 20 lakhs.

- After another 3 years (i.e., 6 years total), it grows to Rs. 40 lakhs.

- After 9 years, it becomes Rs. 80 lakh, and so on.

The exponential growth of your money continues over time. If this cycle continues for 30 years, your original investment doubles **10 times.**

Chapter - 10
How Does Rs. 10 Lakh Become Rs. 100 Crore?

Here's the simple math:

- Start with Rs. 10 lakhs.

- After 3 years, it's Rs. 20 lakhs.

- After 6 years, it's Rs. 40 lakhs.

- After 9 years, it's Rs. 80 lakhs.

- After 12 years, it's Rs. 1.6 crore.

- After 15 years, it's Rs. 3.2 crore.

- After 18 years, it's Rs. 6.4 crore.

- After 21 years, it's Rs. 12.8 crore.

- After 24 years, it's Rs. 25.6 crore.

- After 27 years, it's Rs. 51.2 crore.

- After 30 years, it's Rs. 102.4 crore.

Thus, by investing at a rate of 22% per year, your original investment of Rs. 10 lakhs will grow to over Rs. 100 crores in 30 years. This is the magic of compounding, and the reason why investing early and consistently in high-growth assets can create unimaginable wealth over time.

Chapter - 11
Achieving a 22% Annual Growth Rate: Is It Realistic?

At first glance, a 22% annual return may seem difficult to achieve. It's far higher than the returns of traditional, low-risk investments like bank deposits, bonds, or even the broad stock market indices. For context, the Sensex—one of India's benchmark stock indices—has historically grown at an average annual rate of about **16%**. While this growth is still significant, it's much lower than the 22% required to achieve the kind of results outlined above.

However, achieving a 22% return per year is **not impossible**, and it's where strategic investing can make a difference. Here are a few ways you can aim for higher returns:

1. Investing in High-Growth Companies

One of the keys to achieving 22% annual growth is to find companies with the potential to rapidly scale their earnings. These are typically **growth stocks**—companies that reinvest their profits into expanding their business rather than paying out dividends. These companies might be in emerging industries such as technology, e-commerce, healthcare, or renewable energy.

If you identify companies with strong business models, leadership teams, and market potential, you can ride the wave of their growth and benefit from their profit increases. The critical factor here is the ability to identify these growth stocks early, before they become mainstream.

2. Focus on Compounding and Long-Term Holding

The key to achieving the 22% return isn't necessarily about finding the next big stock every year. Instead, it's about **holding onto your investments for the long term** and allowing compounding to work its magic. Even when stock prices fluctuate, the value of your investment continues to grow as the company reinvests profits and gains market share. By **reinvesting dividends and profits**, you ensure that your money continues to work for you.

3. Diversification and Asset Allocation

While investing in individual high-growth stocks can yield substantial returns, it's also important to **diversify** across different sectors and asset classes. This will reduce risk while still giving you access to high-growth opportunities. Balancing between high-risk, high-return investments (like stocks in emerging sectors) and lower-risk, stable assets (like bonds or blue-chip stocks) can help smooth out fluctuations in the short term and position you for long-term gains.

4. Participating in the Indian Growth Story

India, in particular, is an exciting place for investors looking for high returns. The country's rapid economic growth, young and dynamic workforce, and expanding middle class make it an ideal environment for businesses to thrive. Companies that cater to the domestic market or are poised to become global players can offer outstanding returns to long-term investors. Many top-performing Indian companies—especially in technology, FMCG, and infrastructure—have demonstrated the ability to grow their earnings by 20% or more annually over extended periods.

Chapter - 12
The Fear of Missing the Boat During Market Corrections

One of the most common mistakes investors make is waiting for the "perfect" time to invest. Many investors are afraid to put their money into the market during a **correction**, fearing that prices will continue to fall. However, this approach often leads to missed opportunities, because they **wait for the market to drop further** instead of recognizing the potential in these corrections.

The truth is **corrections are temporary**. They are part of the market's natural cycle. As history has proven time and time again, markets will experience ups and downs, but the overall trend is upward in the long term. **Growth is permanent**. Corrections provide investors with an opportunity to buy quality assets at a discount. When the market rebounds (and it always does), those who invested during the corrections are often the ones who benefit the most.

The key is to stay **focused on the long-term** and avoid getting caught up in short-term fluctuations. The market has always recovered from downturns—whether from the dot-com crash of 2000, the 2008 global financial crisis, or the COVID-19 crash in 2020—and gone on to reach new highs.

Chapter - 13
Why Patience is Crucial?

The magic of turning Rs. 10 lakhs (1 Mn) into Rs. 100 crores (1000 Mn) don't happen overnight. It takes **time, patience, and consistency**. While it's tempting to look for quick wins or attempt to time the market perfectly, the real success comes from staying invested for the long haul. **The longer you stay invested**, the more likely you are to experience the power of compounding and achieve high returns.

Think of it as planting a tree: you don't expect it to bear fruit immediately. It takes years of nurturing, watering, and growth before the tree produces bountiful fruit. Likewise, wealth creation through investments requires a long-term view, consistent strategy, and the discipline to stay the course, even through market corrections.

Conclusion: Achieving Wealth Through Smart Investing

Turning Rs. 10 lakh into Rs. 100 crore in 30 years is a daunting goal, but it's entirely possible with a well-thought-out investment strategy, a focus on high-growth companies, and the ability to stay the course through market corrections. While achieving 22% annual returns may be challenging, it's certainly within the realm of possibility for savvy, long-term investors who make the right choices.

Remember, **"corrections are temporary, and growth is permanent."** If you approach investing with this mindset, stick to a disciplined, long-term strategy, and keep your eyes on the bigger picture, you too can achieve extraordinary wealth over time.

Chapter - 14
Market Shakes? Keep Your Cool

In times of market turbulence, it's easy to feel overwhelmed and tempted to make hasty decisions, but what truly sets successful investors apart is their temperament and perspective. You don't need intricate strategies or cutting-edge investment theories to weather these storms. Instead, what matters most is maintaining a steady hand and staying focused on your long-term goals.

Market declines are often part of the natural cycle, serving as temporary setbacks rather than lasting failures. These dips, while unsettling, provide opportunities for disciplined investors to remain on course and even benefit from a downturn. Historically, patient investors who avoid panic and resist the urge to sell have been rewarded, as markets eventually recover and, over time, continue to grow.

Emotional reactions, such as selling out of fear, often lead to missed opportunities when the market rebounds. The key is **to** see the bigger picture: short-term volatility is just a chapter in a larger story of growth. By keeping a cool head, viewing declines as temporary, and sticking to a well-considered strategy, you are far better positioned to achieve financial success in the long run.

Ultimately, staying calm, committed, and disciplined can make the difference between success and failure in investing.

Chapter - 15
The core principles of wealth-building have stood the test of time.

Despite changes in markets, economies, and financial tools, these foundational strategies remain reliable for creating lasting financial security. They provide a roadmap that, when followed, has proven effective across generations. Here's a closer look at each principle:

1. Start Early: Time is one of the most valuable assets in building wealth. Starting early allows your investments more time to grow through the power of compounding, where the returns on your investments generate their own returns. Even small, regular contributions made in your 20s or 30s can grow significantly over several decades, often more than larger amounts invested later in life. The sooner you start, the more time your money has to work for you, allowing you to accumulate wealth with less pressure to contribute high amounts later on.

2. Save Regularly: Consistency in saving is essential. Building wealth requires regular contributions to your savings and investment accounts, regardless of market conditions or personal circumstances. Developing a disciplined habit of setting aside a portion of your income creates a financial safety net and builds a foundation for future investments. Automating your savings can make this process easier by ensuring you consistently put away money before spending on other items.

3. Invest Carefully: Wise investment choices are crucial. A carefully considered approach to investing involves selecting assets that align with your financial goals, risk tolerance, and timeline. Avoiding impulsive decisions and conducting thorough research or consulting with a financial advisor can help minimize risk. Diversification, or spreading your investments across different asset classes like stocks, bonds, and real estate, can also protect your portfolio against volatility and improve the potential for steady returns over time.

4. Trust Equity: Equities, or stocks, represent ownership in companies and have historically provided some of the highest returns among various asset classes. While they may fluctuate in the short term, equities tend to outperform other investments over long periods, making them essential for wealth building. By consistently investing in quality stocks or equity-based funds, you can benefit from the growth of companies and the economy, which often translates into substantial returns over time.

5. Avoid Unproductive Debt: Debt can be a powerful tool when used wisely, but unproductive debt—such as high-interest credit card debt—drains resources that could otherwise be invested. Managing debt effectively by focusing on paying off high-interest debt and avoiding excessive borrowing can free up cash flow for saving and investing. Maintaining a healthy debt-to-income ratio and being mindful of your spending habits can prevent debt from hindering your financial goals.

6. Think Long Term: Building wealth isn't a short-term project; it requires a long-term mindset. This means setting realistic goals that may take years or even decades to achieve. Market fluctuations are natural, and by maintaining a long-term perspective, you're less likely to make emotionally driven decisions during short-term downturns. Long-term thinking allows you to remain focused on your end goals and avoid the temptation to sell or trade impulsively, which can disrupt your wealth-building efforts.

7. Think Beyond Speculative Impulse: The allure of "quick wins" in speculative investments—like high-risk stocks, cryptocurrencies, or short-term trading—can lead many off course. While some may see rapid returns, speculative investments come with significant risk and potential for loss. Successful wealth-building focuses on steady, reliable growth rather than gambling on market fads. By prioritizing stability over speculation, you're more likely to build sustainable wealth that lasts.

Together, these principles create a comprehensive approach to wealth-building. Each one reinforces the others, creating a financial plan that is resilient against short-term changes in the market. By starting early, saving consistently, investing wisely, trusting in long-term growth, avoiding debt, and steering clear of speculation, individuals can achieve financial security and build wealth that stands the test of time.

Over the past two decades, we have experienced multiple steep market declines, with losses reaching 20-30% or even more. These drops included some of the most significant financial downturns in recent history, such as the 2008 financial crisis and the pandemic-driven plunge in 2020. These events shook global markets, tested investor confidence, and led many to question the stability and future of their investments. For many, these downturns represented periods of heightened uncertainty and anxiety, as they watched their portfolios lose value seemingly overnight.

Yet, despite these challenging times, we find ourselves today in a much stronger position. Those who stayed committed to their investment strategies and didn't panic-sell when the market was at its lowest have seen their wealth multiply several times over. The recovery following each downturn has been powerful, with the markets rebounding to new highs, often within a few years. These recoveries have rewarded those with the patience and resolve to stay invested for the long term, reinforcing the importance of maintaining a steady course even when market conditions seem grim.

It's essential to understand that these periodic declines aren't flaws or malfunctions in the system; rather, they are integral features of the market's natural cycle. While it can be unsettling to experience these downturns, they play a crucial role in creating opportunities for investors.

Each drop allows disciplined investors to purchase high-quality assets at lower prices, essentially getting a "discount" on investments that may have been too expensive before the downturn. Those who recognize this pattern can capitalize on these declines, viewing them not as setbacks but as opportunities for long-term wealth building.

For the disciplined investor, the key lies in understanding that market fluctuations are a normal, expected part of investing. Instead of reacting emotionally to market downturns, these investors remain calm, continuing to invest regularly and strategically during both upturns and downturns. This approach allows them to take advantage of the market's cyclical nature, maximizing returns over time. In this way, enduring and even embracing temporary declines can become a central part of a successful investment strategy, proving time and again that patience, discipline, and a long-term perspective are essential to achieving financial growth.

Chapter - 16
My Real Life Journey

Industry Success Story: How I Built $2 Million in Wealth in 15 Years in the Financial Product Sector

This is my story—how I, a dedicated professional in the financial product industry, achieved the rare feat of amassing a $2 million fortune and creating a steady stream of passive income within less than two decades. Through a combination of discipline, strategic thinking, industry insights, and a passion for helping others secure their financial futures, I transformed my career in finance into a powerful wealth-building journey. Here's a detailed look into how I built significant wealth, developed passive income streams, and achieved financial independence.

1. Starting with a Strong Foundation in Financial Knowledge

I began my journey by gaining a thorough understanding of the financial product industry, focusing on life insurance, mutual funds, Business Continuity plans, and investment vehicles that suited a range of client profiles. By building a solid foundation in these products, I was able to provide clients with sound advice and tailored financial plans, setting the stage for my own financial success. Knowledge became my most valuable asset, helping me not only gain clients' trust but also identify opportunities for personal wealth-building.

2. Consistent and Strategic Investing in High-Growth Assets

With my industry knowledge, I made a personal commitment to invest consistently. Rather than waiting for the perfect time to invest, I started small and continued regularly, taking advantage of compounding returns. Over the years, I focused on high-growth assets, particularly equities, which historically deliver substantial long-term gains. My approach was not to chase short-term trends but to find solid investments with the potential for steady appreciation over the years. This discipline allowed me to grow my portfolio systematically, even during market fluctuations.

3. Diversifying Income Streams for Stability and Growth

I understood that true financial independence comes from multiple income streams. In addition to earning commissions and fees from my financial products business, I began to develop passive income through investments that paid dividends, interest, and rental income. By reinvesting my earnings and gradually expanding my portfolio, I was able to diversify my income sources. This not only protected me during economic downturns but also provided a steady income stream that I could rely on without depleting my core assets.

4. Building a Strong Client Base and Earning Passive Commissions

A critical part of my strategy was to build a loyal client base through excellent service and dependable advice. By genuinely focusing on my clients' financial well-being, I earned repeat business and referrals, which translated into recurring commission income from products like life insurance. Over time, this became a source of passive income, as existing policies generated ongoing commissions without the need for constant new sales. By prioritizing relationships over transactions, I developed a self-sustaining business model where my past efforts continued to yield returns.

5. Maintaining a Long-Term Perspective and Avoiding Speculative Risks

My journey to wealth was marked by my commitment to a long-term perspective. I avoided high-risk, speculative investments that could offer quick gains but also significant losses. Instead, I maintained a conservative approach, focusing on products with a history of stable returns and low volatility. I recognized that building wealth was not about making a single lucrative trade but rather a series of disciplined, strategic moves over many years. My patience allowed me to navigate economic downturns like the 2008 financial crisis and the 2020 market crash without panicking or deviating from my plan.

6. Emphasizing Financial Literacy and Educating Clients

A key component of my success was my commitment to educating clients. I often conducted seminars, webinars, and one-on-one sessions to help clients understand the value of long-term investing, the dangers of debt, and the importance of financial planning. By empowering clients to make informed decisions, I not only strengthened my relationships but also built a reputation as a trusted advisor. This reputation helped me grow my client base and earn referrals, further supporting my business growth and passive income.

7. Leveraging Tax-Advantaged Accounts and Financial Planning Strategies

Throughout my journey, I maximized my returns by strategically using tax-advantaged accounts and financial planning tools. By utilizing retirement accounts, tax-efficient mutual funds, and insurance policies that provided tax benefits, I was able to minimize my tax burden and increase my after-tax returns. My approach to financial planning extended beyond mere investments, incorporating tax management, estate planning, and other strategies that protected my wealth and enhanced its growth.

8. Reinvesting Profits and Allowing Compounding to Take Effect

I understood that the secret to accelerated wealth growth lies in the power of compounding. Instead of withdrawing my profits, I consistently reinvested my earnings back into my portfolio, allowing the returns to generate further returns. This cycle of reinvestment helped my wealth multiply faster, transforming modest early contributions into substantial wealth over time. Compounding, along with disciplined savings and investment habits, became one of the cornerstones of my wealth-building strategy.

9. Staying Adaptable and Embracing Industry Changes

As the financial industry evolved, I adapted by learning about new financial products, digital tools, and market trends. By staying updated, I was able to offer clients innovative solutions and keep my business relevant in a rapidly changing landscape. My adaptability not only helped me retain clients but also provided me with the knowledge to leverage new opportunities for my investments. This flexibility ensured that my strategy remained effective in an industry that is continuously transforming.

10. Achieving Financial Independence and Inspiring Others

After 15 years of dedicated work, strategic investing, and disciplined saving, I reached my goal of $2 million in wealth. Beyond the monetary achievement, I also created a reliable stream of passive income that covered my living expenses, allowing me to become financially independent. My story is not only one of personal success but also a source of inspiration for others in the financial product industry and those looking to build wealth.

My journey is a testament to the power of disciplined investing, client-centred service, and long-term planning. My approach shows that wealth-building is not about overnight success but about consistent efforts, wise choices, and a vision that spans decades. Through my achievements, I demonstrate that financial independence is attainable for anyone willing to commit to proven principles and stay the course.

We Eagerly Await Your Review

Your journey has just begun, and your perspective matters to us. This book was crafted to provide readers with guidance, hope, and practical steps for overcoming challenges and moving toward a brighter, more fulfilling life.

Your insights and reflections help us understand the impact of this message and contribute to the ongoing conversation about personal transformation and resilience. We would be honoured to hear how the book resonates with you and how it influences your journey.

So, as you turn each page and reflect on its ideas, please consider sharing your review. We eagerly await your thoughts and the opportunity to learn how this book has inspired or empowered you on your path forward.